TODAY, I FOUND THIS ROSE...

ORIGINAL EDITION

.

Today,
I Found
This Rose...

Poetry By
Cedric L. Jones

Thespis Books | New York

Thespis Books
New York, NY
www.ThespisBooks.com

First Edition: June 2018

Jones, Cedric L., author

Cover design by Cedric L. Jones
Vintage Roses via Graphics Fairy (public domain)
Proofreading by Kimberly M. Moore and Alison Marts

ISBN-13:   13: 978-1-7320357-0-6
ISBN-10:   1-7320357-0-9

Printed in the United States of America.

CONTENTS

Thank You!

To the friends who, over wine and snacks, under the stars in Central Park, before a screening of *The Godfather*, became (almost willingly) my "focus group" - thank you: Isabel, Jamie, Ali, Bryan, Jess, Ed; and thank you, Pablo and Ann. Kimberly, dear sis, you get me.

Thanks to my mother, who said "*So what? I already knew that*" when I came out, sobbing like a lost child.

Thanks to Billy and Jermaine who went dancing with me at Scorpio Lounge when I came out, running around like a child with a new toy, and for the dining room table conversation. Your friendships molded me.

Thank you for choosing this book. As artists, we lay things down without ever knowing if anyone will pick them up.

And of course, thanks to all my loves – past, present, and yet to come.

A Note From the Author:

As a kid, I dreamed of one day falling in love. It was supposed to be the magic solve to all things wrong in the world, just like in the movies. Eventually, I did fall in love — a few times.

It turns out love doesn't always end in happily ever after, and the credits don't scroll neatly over a tune. Love is not a love poem. It is a befuddling, intense, ever-changing beast. It can wake us in the morning and make us cry ourselves to sleep at night.

Once, an old friend shared with me his tale of betrayal and the subsequent heartbreak, and I found in someone else my same need for bachelorhood as a means of self-preservation.

It's not that I don't still love *love*. I do! I eagerly await my next great romantic tragedy. It has been the lifeblood of the poetic genre since antiquity. Many a great poet has fallen dead on his/her pen in the name of passion. For, while there are many odes to falling in love, don't we poets have more fun falling out of it?

We tap along to the old-fashioned *"pack your things and go 'cause I never loved you anyway"* songs and play them over and over. What's more cathartic than ripping out your own heart and wringing out the tears?

When friends ask why I haven't found *the one*, I assure them that I found *the one...*and the second *one*, and the third *one* after that. I've never had trouble falling in love. Staying there? That's a different tune altogether. In the meantime, I've gathered some poems that celebrate the romance, heartbreak and, sometimes, humor of relationships. Most are my testimony, some told to me by others, and some whispered by strangers I've yet to meet.

I hope you find something in *Today, I Found This Rose...* that makes you tap along or, better yet, wring out your heart.

Cedric L. Jones
New York City, January 2018

Today,
I Found
This Rose...

I.

Lying beside you,
my heart expands with
moonlight.
Loving makes me glow.

Souvenirs

I gather all the
bits and pieces of you
and wear them like a coat
—every birthday card
and silly poem
and every note
on which you wrote
cute and cuddly come-ons.

Take This, My Vow

Take this, my vow, and wed with me
Tonight beneath yon willow tree
And sovereign moon that glows above,
Near rivers reminiscent of
Cyprus, throne of Aphrodite.

We'll take our oath on bended knee:
Us. You and I. He and He. We.
Create me as god of my love.
Take this, my vow.

Love! That sweet name I grant to thee!
Come! Share sweet sips of heavenly
Ambrosia's nectar, borne by doves,
And evermore be legend loves
Wed in faith, trust, and harmony.
Take this, my vow.

Perfect Snow

There are times when, during a tranquil snowfall, you reach out your palm in hopes of capturing the perfect snowflake.

Please, don't melt.

Your Handsomeness

Your handsomeness
is not in your face alone,
but in your hands
that clench.
It's in your neck
that pulses with veins
as you strain
against injustice.

It's in your fist
that fights for freedom.
It's in your awkward feet
when we dance.
It's in your clean pressed shirt
and your rugged denim pants.

Your handsomeness
is your grace
as you offer your chair,
your gaze
as you stare
from across the room.

It's in the air that
lingers when you've
gone too soon.
It's in that
Aw-shucks smile
that makes me swoon.

It's in your breath
as you speak
softly, sweetly to me.

Your handsomeness
is in my eyes
when I see you.
It's in all the things you are,
all the things you do.

No, your handsomeness
is not in your face alone.
I swear you are beautiful
down to the bone.

When you are
close to me, I think
I'm handsome too
—for a while,
and I too smile
that *Aw-shucks* smile.

I Try Beauty

I'd rather stimulate you with my mind.
Some say I'm well informed and widely read.
But to my witticisms you are blind.
Perhaps it's pulchritude that turns your head.

Disregarding all my aspirations,
I diet to a fraction of myself.
Famished for regard and admiration,
I've banished pride and breeding to a shelf.

While I've turned from scholarly ambitions
And cultivated fashion to an art,
This I ponder as a mathematician:
I muse it's beauty that may jolt your heart!

My wisdom has been trumped by vanity.
So, I try beauty. That may be the key.

Rainstorm

The sky is cracking
but the world inside is quiet.
Here, it's just you and I.
We lie
and listen to
the drumming on the panes
and fall like rain
in love again, and again.

You Are Amazing

You are coffee essence
dark chocolate eyes
skin as smooth as milk.

It seems you are made of silk
when I am close to you
like clouds against the sky.
I need to grasp why
you don't know you are beautiful
while I'm dutiful
in telling you so.

Lover,
this is not a show
to render you unclothed.
I already know
that you are amazing.

Eromenos

On archaic isle
baptized in the tears of Aphrodite,
as Hephaestion to Alexander
Patroclus to Achilles
am I to you
in fields where windflowers grow.

While other men speculate,
lovers know.

It's Warmer in the Sunshine

It's warmer in the sunshine, love. Don't bathe
yourself in wasted tears at night. Lie dry in
morning bright. Open to suck the rays as a
grateful bud blossoms in delicious light
illuminating below as above.
It's warmer in the sunshine love,
he told me.

DADA: Love Reconstructed

I rip the poem you have left for me on the kitchen table beside the coffee ring into jagged pieces and lay out the scraps to see if I can read beyond the words.

> *[cloudless eyes*
> *all that's best*
> *below*
> *starry]*

Through heart shaped vines, the early sun casts jungle shapes on the travertine tile where the cat stretches and mews for his breakfast. I rearrange the nouns, adjectives, sound out the verbs, the consonants, elongate the vowels

> *[that brow*
> *this mellowed*
> *dark and bright glow]*

to find sense in all of this sensibility and security, this meter. I pour kibble for my feline friend and again try to discern what lies within the gift you have left me. I squint to find something hidden there.

[and o'er spent days
in pure a mind at peace
tender heart
goodness smiles bright]

It baffes me, this rising early, this leaving
love notes, poems, kisses warming my day.

[Heaven win
whose skies
in beauty like
the night dwelling place
innocent]

Through the blur of heavy, tear-laden
lashes and lingering sleep I see the torn,
scattered bits and I read out your love for
me.

On Cold Nights

There are times on chill May nights
when the bedroom window has
been left open, but I am too
fatigued to shut it. I think that if I
could just concentrate on the
business of falling asleep, the cold
will go away. Dismayed, I grow
frigid. The winter bedclothes have
been put away too soon. A gust of
cold permeates the room.
Gooseflesh covers me like
sprinkled cinnamon and, just as I
begin to shiver, you arrive to wrap
me in an embrace, fold me into you
as cozy and content as rose vines
sunbathing in July.

Addendum to Afternoon Delight

The university clock tower shivers and churns out a peal that reverberates through acres of ancient trees and stone as you pour out the last of your inhibitions in drops. Flows with it the tiniest *I Love You,* which roars through me as brush fire in a valley sick with drought.

I Love You As Sunlight Loves the Dawn

My love is but a trite phenomenon
compared to ecstasy that angels know.
Still, I love you as sunlight loves the dawn.

No, science has no theorem why this spawns
to grow like some disease. Yet this they know:
my love is but a *trite* phenomenon.

Yes, war and strife and misery rage on,
and poetry won't strike a heartening blow.
Still, I love you as sunlight loves the dawn.

The brave have braver things to act upon,
while faint of heart is all I'll ever know.
My love is but a trite *phenomenon*.

I shan't assume the polish of Don Juan,
with pockets deep or brawn physique to show.
Still, I *love* you as sunlight loves the dawn.

I cherish you! Forgive me if I fawn
or smother you with tenderness. I know
my love is but a trite phenomenon.
Still, I love you as sunlight loves the dawn.

A Walk Along the Beach

Perhaps I am prone to needless
jealousy, but I believe
Mother Nature may be more in
love with you than I,
the way the stormy sky
stops the rain, shushes restless
thunder,
submissively parts lush clouds.

The tumultuous ocean calms to
tenderly caress your bare feet,
reaches up
to stroke your calves, your knees,
your thigh.

I watch when sand, newly dry,
smooth and swept by doting wind,
takes you into its bosom. Then,
seabirds softly serenade songs
with just your name in refrain
as sunbeams sweetly kiss your
bronze skin
again and again
as I thought only I could.

Conquest

Were the angels studious to make thee,
Or is this thrall a case of happenstance?
Is it witchcraft that you use to shake me
From my resolve to not give love a chance?

You eviscerate my steadfast defense,
Wielding a smile that gleams as does a sword.
Pierce me! I shall bleed out my resistance.
Then, spill the seeds of ardor from my core.

I capitulate to your libido
And pledge to do exactly as you please.
Strip away my righteousness and ego.
Rebuild me as a temple for your needs.

Come! Claim the vestal prize that thou hast won.
Take glory, Knight. Your conquest is now done.

Find Me

I've left traces of
myself for you to find
in peach trees down below
the Mason Dixon Line,
in French Canadian ports
and along the Gulf of Mexico,
also down in St. Thomas
on the backs of green iguanas,
and in bus depots
from 42nd to Gowanus.
On a postcard
on Broad Street
in the Carolinas I wrote:

     Dear "The One,"
     Find me.

II.

Craving your embrace
I take alternate lovers.
Imitations break.

They Tell You

They say that the eyes
are the windows to
the soul.
But how do I get to your heart?
'Though I'm lost in your eyes
for hours on end,
I haven't a clue where to start.

They tell you there's someone
for everyone.
They tell you that dreams
do come true.
So why am I lying in bed with another,
but all the while
dreaming of you?

Chopper

Hey Chopper —
buzzing like a highway bee
me stuck to your back
red and black

Slow down
and let me remember.

You were
attracted to the sweetness
of my sweet tang
sweet thing
and I was enamored
of your brute.

I want to ride
hard metal
between our thighs
fast and furious
down Peachtree Road
like we used to do.

Now, every night
the clock ticks
in the hall,
      and I'm missing you.

As Bluebird Sings
To A Dove

The fervid Bluebird
dances with joy, for his muse
is the graceful Dove.

Bluebird trills gaily,
tossing happiness skyward.
Dove coos demurely.

I am but this beast,
featherless, wingless, inept—
Circumspect! Muted.

On the Queens Bound
M Train

Five-ten

scruffy
duck shoes

Peppermint.

Thick mop
kind eyes

thighs

Those glasses.
that nose.

He bumped into me as the M train lurched, his
smile an apology I gladly accepted.
He went back to his e-book as
I read him all over.

wrinkled shirt
backpack

Smudges

Tight grip
thick

fingertips.

Lips.

I Knew You Weren't There

Somewhere,
down where the truth grows
twisting into serpentine roots
nourished by darkness and moist,
I knew your soft eyes
did not await mine. I knew
your voice was as distant and untouchable
as the shadow of the moon.

Yet, I lumbered on
past Harlem, due north
hunched over a book
about a lover, stealing glances
at the lovers in the corner and,
all the time—
I knew you weren't there.

I could have been spared the
pitying sigh of the young hostess
and the bartender pushing me
a drink I didn't need if I'd
closed the book and crossed the platform
to the downtown train,
but I remained.

They say we only want
what we can't have.
I dared not take the chance
of missing your stolen glance
or nervous repartee. Still—

I knew you weren't there.

Mardi Gras Beads

I never knew
You had it in you.

Gold and purple wearing
Drunk and swearing—
Showing it all for me
Giving it all to me.

I love the way you move
Swinging those beads
Dancing with joy
Music box boy.

But I digress
From the cruelty of your jest
And the intent of your deeds...

Let's dip around this corner
From your wholesome masquerade.
You can tell me it's your first time
And then lie about your age.

I knew it was a party
When you caught my eye and lingered.
You licked your lips, full wet
And traced my palm with your forefinger.

We celebrate Fat Tuesday.
You fulfill my wicked needs.
Here I'll wear a mask of truth
And tie you down with purple beads.

Like gluttons, we shall feast
With sweaty palms and heavy breath.
When there's sex and wine aplenty,
There's no need to starve to death.

You may sate yourself with me
And I shall treat you like a gent
Nibbling sugar coated almonds. Then—
     I'll give you up for Lent.

I'll untie you at the dawn
And send you far, far from the dark.
We shan't speak about the fire.
We'll not dwell upon the sparks.

I could never see myself
The way I saw you next, dear sir.
It was noontide on Ash Wednesday.
You were hand in hand with her.

Between Two Chairs

He stood between
two cream-colored chairs,
French dripping
from his tongue, gathering
in pools like fallen petals.

What makes a man
full of swagger and boast
shrivel and crumble
like dry brown toast?

He said he stood
between two roads
and could not choose
which to take—
suspended in nautical twilight
between the night and day.

He asked:

> *"How can one live like that,*
> *with his compass cracked*
> *and a two-sided map?"*

Both worlds bring comfort
and both give much joy
to the Curious Boy.

So I drew the curtains closed
and folded his rumpled clothes
and wiped away his nervousness
with the palm of my hand.

I turned a curious boy
into a wiser man.

The next night,
he sat in the other chair
and on his lap was
She, in her cream-colored dress,
with her long, pretty hair.

Yes, French still
dripped from his tongue,
gathering in pools
around my feet.

But wise men don't tell —
and empty chairs don't speak.

I'm In Love
(With Your Best Friend)

When you next decide to arrive
late while we wait,
dinner cold, growing old

together, we may decide
it's better
you don't arrive at all.

Someone Else's Guy

All the charm
That ever was
Gathers in that smile.

I'd love to
Kiss and cuddle you,
Hold you for a while.

You're an impish little giant
And so tender I could cry
But, 'though I do adore you:
You're someone else's guy.

Each time
You're close to me
I feel our souls connect.

I'm buzzing
Like a bee and you're
The flower I'd inject.

You're sugar in my coffee.
You're the apple of my eye
But, while you stick like honey,
You're someone else's guy.

Were I to stay another day,
I would be sure to pine away.

And, while you are a part of me,
I know that we shall never be.

Thus, from your gaze, I must depart
To disengage my longing heart.

You're the spring rain that wets me
As so much for you I cry.
While I honestly do love you:

You're someone else's guy.

Our Beloved

It seems we have something in common.

The way you look at him
is the way I feel.

We giggle at the same joke
cover the same mouth
bat the same eye.
We like the same guy.

You make me your confidant
        (breaking my heart).
I give you advice as bland
as the taste in my mouth.

I want to despise, but
I understand why

we bat the same eye
cover the same smile
do anything we're asked to do. You
and I, we like the same guy.

Why?
The way he locks eyes
when you speak,

the way, when you embrace,
he presses your cheek?

Is it the way he makes you feel
like you're the only other person in the room
that makes you swoon?

What—
he makes you feel that way too?

We giggle at the same joke
we clear the same throat
we palpitate and sigh

all over the same guy.

Solomon

We wasted those
Quiet streets where
No one would
Have watched us.

I would have
Slipped into the
Shadows with you
And fallen to my knees
If you'd only said *please*.

We could have become one,
Solomon.

Instead,
We traded
Nervous laughter
Like playing cards

As you led me
Back to civilization.

I am the dealer
Who lost control of the deck.

Candy From a Stranger

Look both ways,
   hold hands on the left.

I took candy from a stranger
   with my right

ran with scissors
   down a hall

slick with secrets
   and took long rides

behind tinted windows
   tongue wagging lies.

Sex may be sin—
   but love would be demise.

Played with matches
   kissed the burn

feasted until sated.
   Unwrapped candy. Tasted.

Legs

I know you as you
stand in darkness

straight back
straight legs

who have never
known monkey bars
swings
scars

milky white
against my brown toast
melted butter.

Your long lanate legs
speak to me
against my ears
like wispy worm silk.

I answer back:
yes.

Scorpio: Prelude

I fell in love once a week on the dance floor in a
gay club in Charlotte, NC after the Sunday
night drag show when I was supposed to be at
the straight bar down the street. The music, the
men, the steam curling through the vents like
Circe's song were alluring, sweet: Apples. In
our tight shirts and tighter jeans, we knew we
were grown. Yet, we always went home alone.

Scorpio: The Dance

That beat beats down
That underground sound

We sway, gyrate
And pop nonstop

On the dance floor.
Gimme gimme gimme more.

You against my
Backside. We slide

And move our hips and slip
Into the groove.

Dude--
I love the way you move!

Sip cold Zima and cherry

Very hot sweat drops
Like diamonds from the sopped

Shirt you take off
And I'm a jewel thief

Grabbing you
And pressing you close to me.

Baby, can you feel that heat?

Beat box hip-hop music stops
As the DJ plays pause for the cause.

It's last call for alcohol.

You ain't got to go home
But you got to get the hell up out of here!

Write down your number
And finish that beer.

We've got one last
Dance and chance

To let me let you get me
Out of my pants.

Turn me around and let me know
What you know down below.

But—
My friends wait by the door
'Cause it's time to go.

It's the end of our night
Out at Scorpio.

You Leave Me Breathless

Can't catch on
to the rhythm.

      Damn it!

Think! Think!
Focus!

      Catch your breath
      or he might notice.

Drowning in dryness!

My lungs betray me
because you touched me.

But you don't catch on
to the death of me.

I'm good at what I do—
hiding my affection for you.

Yet, the sly moon that hangs
above can see
how your charm asphyxiates me:

The feel of your fur
against my cheek
as we part

that hand
on my lower back,
jolting my heart

Your smile as you wave
after saying goodbye

Your lingering scent
that makes me die!

I grin like an imbecile
watching you leave

I cling to the lamp post and,
as my chest heaves,

I pull at the air
settle down...

and breathe.

Walk of Shame?

I'm walking along, head held high
as he dries on my thigh.

Straight down Main Street
I don't miss a beat
and I feel no shame
for what I did
or from whence I came.

I walk with confidence
—my backside
swinging like a pendulum
as I think of him.

I was right.
That one night stand
didn't even last the night.

I nod to passersby,
Hey, how you?
Sometimes it seems they
may know what I do.

But if they knew
who he was then they
wouldn't throw shade.
They'd throw me a
goddamned parade!

They would beg me
to tell it
again and again

And then he...
  And then he...

Walk of shame?
Ha!
Honey, hell no!
That ain't my game!

Not everyone can boast
of a conquest so fine—
but, for two hours,
twenty-five minutes,
and fifty-seven seconds
he was mine, all mine!

I will write it down
in my little black book
how he shook,
given over to ecstasy
because of me.

Me!
Strutting down Main Street
with my head held high
feeling like I
could spread my legs
like wings
and fly!

Whiskey in Your Mustache

You smell of cigarettes, you randy man and
I am trying to understand
just what you want...
so I can become that. You've got

whiskey in your mustache
and tobacco in your teeth.
I like that you're the devil
with an angel underneath.

Take another sour sip of sin
and breathe on me nonstop.
You've a twitchy eye
and wandering speech
that never seems to stop.
I roll you over in my mind
to let you be on top.

You want another round?
Sure!
It wears resistance down
and puts that

whiskey in your mustache
and confessions in your mouth.
You say you wanted freedom,
that's the reason you walked out.
You talk about the love you lost,
but you don't seem bereft with

whiskey in your mustache
and the lies that taint your breath.

Like mumblety-peg
Russian roulette
Cocaine and crystal meth,
You intrigue me and
excite me!
Man, you scare me half to death!

My!
You do beguile with that smirk
so like a smile.
It makes me want to quit at life
and linger for a while.

But—
it seems the night is through.
No!
I won't go home with you.

I shall drain my glass
and wring this moment
'til there's nothing left

and leave with whiskey in my brain
and your mustache on my breath.

Poet Lights Candles at Midnight

I light candles at midnight and speak your name. Your voice is plain like lead, but those eyes that see, they say so much.

I hum jazz songs to summon you. Spellbound, you lay down your truth as bare as your feet. I tune you until you are pitch perfect.

"Hold me close and hold me fast..."

I conjure poet progenitors from a time when silence was truth to help me understand why I shall never feel the confidence I felt in the hours before I met you, with your eyes that see. Hart Crane condoles with me. We poets drown in the cliché of unrequited love and rhyme.

Shall I compare thee?

I speak to my candles, carve my bidding into their wax, anoint the wicks, the crevices and my skin and my nails and my lips with oil and musk.

At dusk, I put on my *never-have-I-ever* mask to meet you for drinks, stop up my tongue with wine. For, if I should pour it all out like nectar I'd starve the bees, topple this carefully built house of tarot cards, leave us both exposed. My confessions are leaves gathered from shaken limbs and swept away.

Near midnight, I laugh at your tales and your jokes and I feel I shall choke on the pheromones spilling from you in dense fumes, thickening the air like roux. As the unspoken between us swells we are quick to find distraction:

Singing in the backs of taxis careening trough Midtown

Sailing past the statue of liberty, taking selfies of self-pity

Pretending not to care.

Your moods creep like seasons.
Mine rip like storms and rain down
rose quartz crystals on a cluttered
altar where, when licked by
moonlight, they blaze aflame.

I light candles at midnight and
speak your name.

Thorny Roses

The rose bouquet
is rife with thorns.
I love it just the same.
I bleed from its caresses and
I call it by your name.

I press your roses to my heart.
They gouge me to the core.
When I drown myself in tears,
I'll leave them on the shore.

III.

Our moonlit desire
vapored with the
morning dawn.
We were but shadows.

Today,
I Found This Rose...

Today I found this
Flower pressed between the sheets
Like we used to love.
Given to me long ago,
It crumbled like our passion.

The Corners of My Mind

I sift through
my memories
like a picker
in a landfill
and turn them over,
every piece of rubbish
I find —
broken cassette tapes
cracked television
bent screen door
spiral notebooks.
Souvenirs.
I circle around a pile
of neatly stacked regrets
to find you there naked,
shivering in a corner.

Damaged Goods

Rattling around
in this impregnable box
stamped with destinations like
Deep South
Big City
West Side of Hell
smudged with the fingerprints
of ones who didn't
handle with care
and silently screaming
to each passerby

deliver me!

Your True Love

Your true love went away.
Perhaps it's not so true after all.
If so, it would have stayed
And never would have strayed.

Dear Estranged Lover

I checked the mail at noontime
and you'd sent nothing
to my address.
So, when the trash truck
came at three,
I sent your things Express.

You're Throwing Me Away

I am possessive of you because you
own me. Yet, you don't know how
to use me: place me on a shelf to be
dusted, stuffed and cuddled,
crumple me up, put me outside on
Tuesday to be recycled, plastic
melted and malleable to your will,
or give me to another

Lover, I am stamped with
barcodes, an expiration date, and a
warranty label,
but handle with care.

Giovanni's Room

I shut myself up in Giovanni's room to see if I can understand how he feels about David leaving him and I realize we both love the same books, our shirts are the same size. We sleep on the same side of the bed and we both have the same tune stuck in our heads. *La Vie en Rose*. We sit in the same spot on the edge of the unmade bed and watch the door for David *(only, I don't call you David)* to enter the room. We both die much too soon, pining for a world where roses bloom. We plead with one voice, Giovanni and I, share the same tears. As you shuffle away with the same gait as *Daveed*, we drown in the same wine, our sorrows. We toast Hella.

I shut myself up in Giovanni's room to see if I can understand how he feels about David leaving him, and I realize we both love.

Note: Inspired by the 1956 novel of the same name by James Baldwin.

I've Picked a Paper Bouquet

My first love was a rose,
soft to kiss and sweet of scent
but prickly to the touch.
I don't think of him too much.
He was difficult to trust.

Next, my pretty Dandelion
swore he'd never stray.
But, with the changing
of the breeze,
he promptly blew away.

I swear the flower in between,
malcontent since seed,
had to be a weed.
I tended to
his every mood.
He never seemed to bloom.

The Calla Lily, so demure,
was innocence undone.
So puissant was his need
he'd thrust that spathe at anyone.

So now, I've paper flowers
for my dashing new bouquet.
They do not go astray
and, best of all—they won't decay.

This Relationship

In the darkness
you tell me you love me
and of your regrets.
At daybreak
you start anew —
ripping and tearing,
scraping and mauling
my emotions.

Alone,
your eyes are full of me.
You are mine.
In company
you start anew —
pushing and torturing,
denying and turning
away from me.

This moment
I am happy
and all unrest is gone.
Later,
I may start anew —
sobbing and crying,
fainting and dying
over you.

This is
perhaps
an unhealthy
relationship.

The Same

You don't see me as you used to.
You don't smile and say my name.
You don't have to speak to tell me
you're not loving me the same.

I find solace in your silence.
I imagine what you'd say.
If you speak, you're sure to tell me
you're not loving me the same.

Were I honest, I could tell you
that it hurts me to the core.
When you push and pull away from me,
I love you all the more.

Yet, I shall not play the victim
or assign a needless blame.
In the natural course of nature,
you're not loving me the same.

You don't shower me with kisses.
I'm alone and soaked with pain.
So, I'll lie to make you happy:

"I'm not loving you the same."

The Call

The floor is still sticky
with your footprints
when you call to tell me
you're not coming home.

And I lament:

> *Is he smarter than me?*
> *Prettier than me?*
> *Richer than me?*

Finally, I realize
it really doesn't matter
what you're doing
on the other end
of the phone.

What matters is that
I disconnect
and make this life
my own.

DADA: Love Deconstructed

I clean out corners with dusty broom
straws
swish, sweep
scraps

> *[shade soft*
> *nameless sky*
>
> *beauty*
>
> *dark dwelling place mellowed*
> *peace in days*
> *peace in days]*

gather in a pile amidst coffee grounds and
kibble.

I squint to find something there.

Instead, the dust gathers in my head, in my
throat, in my sinuses and I sneeze with the
last effort I will ever make for what was
once a beautiful morning.

I Wrote This Poem For You

I've written verse for paramours
whose names I've long forgotten;
For whom, I swore in mawkish prose,
I'd always be besotted.

Yet, never have I from my pen
composed an edict true
to tell you how I feel. Therefore,
I wrote *this* poem for *you*...

Alas! I shall not tell thee that
thou art more fair than gold.
For gold, in aging, keeps its glow
while humans, well—grow old.

I'd add up my solicitude,
  but figures seem to lie.
No sweet red rose, nor tender buds—
  for bouquets tend to die.

No! Browning, Keats and Byron shan't,
  with fawning, guide my hand!
I dreamed of romance as a boy.
  I have become a man.

As the moths who came and went,
  you're sure to bid adieu.
In lieu of wasted sentiment,
  I wrote *this* poem for *you*.

Photograph

You have become such
a photograph.

Magic men conjure,
Golden Boys bring pause
but, in real life
there was you—
graceful and beautiful
with just the right
touch
and just the right
touch of sincerity.

Missing you is like
missing a part of myself
that may never return—
something familiar,
comfortable,
without question,
but with regret.

Do I still love you,
or am I in love
with being in love?

Prelude to a Breakup

I try to count the ways I love you as
one counts sheep. I lie awake.
There is no plausible reason why I
cling to you like pollen on a bee's
foot, knowing there is no way to
configure my bird, your fish, our
nest into any combination that may
last.

...Until It's Gone

She's on the radio
crooning all the words
I should have said to you
oh, so long ago—

"Go ahead and go."

Her free verse frees my mind
and pairs so well with wine,
I'm tipsy.

I listen to her voice soar
and I feel that Diva's pain.
I swore I'd never
let you make me
feel this way again.

> *"I loved you in all the right ways
> and honey, it was wrong."*

You won't appreciate my love
until it's gone.

There goes that part
where the saxophone starts
to wail.

The piano imparts
a broken heart,
while the strings
pick up the tale.

Her voice dips low
with the bass trombone
as Diva slays the tune.

I swirl my wine
while keeping time
and raise my glass to you,
lift my voice to
sing of our love
in the swell
of an old torch song:

> *"You won't know what you have
> until it's gone."*

Our Dirty Little Secret

Why do I workshop you
when I know you
won't be real?

I know the deal.

I struggle to find the truth
and you struggle to keep it

and, with it keep me
your dirty little secret.

We walk across the stage
but cross too slow
since we both know

we're biding time
until you find yours
and I find mine.

and in the time
that is the meantime,

we'll rehearse it and repeat it.

Then, I'll make you
my dirty little secret.

Sometimes we are so cruel
with words we do not mean—

words that are grown
from shades of...evergreen;

Words so sticky
they caulk and bind like glue.

I wear them for our friends
but if they only knew...

We take our bows
and exit separate wings at night.

Later, steal together
somewhere shady, out of sight

to make another desperate vow.
I know we'll never keep it.

One day we'll tell the tale
of our

dirty

little

secret.

Dead Flowers

Roses are red,
so why am I blue?

Flowers lose their color
when they die
as did the love I had for you.
I know my love was true
because well—
    here I am holding
    dead flowers.

But after wilting
comes the brittle hardness of decay
that started on the day
you went away and
gave a marriage bouquet
to another
my summer lover.

Now, I reckon
those flowers are also dead
and losing color
like the memory
of the day you came to me,
hand outstretched and said:

"Roses are red..."

Congratulations
on Becoming a Father

Remember the night
you punched a hole in the wall
so jagged I thought
it was my heart?

How when my friends
came to play guitar,
you stopped being shy and stayed,
talked and gave away
all the laughter
that was meant for only me?

When I packed my things for NYC
you were nowhere to be found.
You were somewhere down
in Florida
making the last money you could
before you were scheduled for
deportation.

Now, you are back
across the sea,
far away from me,
looking new and shiny
with someone new and tiny
to call you Daddy.

Wringing Out My Heart

Because drip-dry did not work,
because I am made of flesh and bone,
not the stretched cotton of the airbrushed
        t-shirt he left behind

not carnations, nor greeting cards
        that burn when lit
not silk pajamas worn on vacation days,
        holidays, anniversaries,
letters forwarded from addresses long
        forgotten
not one shiny black kimono, ankle length,
        seam come undone or

empty cologne bottles
emails bounced back
or guilt.

Because I am heavy, sopping with memories
        that do not drip-dry
because I am made of flesh and sinew, bone
        and ego

I am wringing out my heart.

And when I am done
I shall be an empty vessel waiting
        to soak up every bit of

salacious
sweet
sentiment

you wish to pour into me.

Letting Go

I soaked you up like flowers in sunshine and drank your kisses like rain. Blossomed. Rolled around hallways like marbles full of color and lofty dreams, making love with college on my breath and saying *I love you* with tenacity in the timbre of my voice. Each tale began and ended with your name as I forgot my own. My devotion spilled out, drunken poetry on parchment that I wrapped around my tender heart when you finally broke it, leaping from shadows, boogie-man to my emotions, and I was still afraid of the dark when time sifted through my fingers; But I held on to the memory of you like you were the last vestige of my youth.

I held on to you like a liar holds on to the truth; Like a child, expecting a mythical being to leave him coins, holds on to a tooth.

I held on to you like parts of an antique vase, trying to piece you back together in my mind.

I held on to you like a wino holds on to wine, all rumpled paper bag, no glass, swearing that each sip of your memory would be my last!

I held on to you with both hands broken, bandaged from beating my fists against the walls around my heart just to let you in. I held on to you like a preacher holds on to sin.

I held on to you like a magician holds on to his greatest trick and, when you disappeared into a plume of cobalt smoke – I held on to the fumes.

I held on to you like you hold
that boy in this picture with his
eyes like mine and his smile like
mine and the skin that used to be
mine. If I could have held on to my
youth, I'd still be holding you.

But, if I told you that I
remember you, it would be a lie.

Time has erased the impression of
your embrace. I don't recall the
warmth of you against me, the
notes of your laughter. Twenty
years later, I don't recall the scent
of your skin, your taste. I don't
recall you ever saying my name…
or loving me.

I held on to you like an aged dancer holds on to a scrapbook, moving in a silent room, no music, mimicking a curtain call, make-believe applause, forgetting aching muscles, swollen feet and recalling only the melody.

I traded sticky photographs for real life and settling down for empty nights. I'm still unsettled. If you could have given me ever after, I would have given you everything.

I held on to you while you were letting go and, twenty years later I still refer to you as my ex when you're really just somebody that I used to know.

It is only now, looking at this photograph of you with that boy that would have been me that I finally realize: I let go of you long, long ago —the only thing I have ever truly held on to is the memory of the *me* that used to love.

At Seventy-Five

I sometimes wonder if, at seventy-
five, I'll miss you or even
remember us

> *(like that one guy from that one*
> *time I'm already starting to*
> *forget).*

I sometimes wonder if I'll know
anything at all.

> *(It frightens me, all the*
> *memories I haven't made that I*
> *may forget).*

I sometimes wonder if I'll regret,
at seventy-five, not giving you a
second chance when you brought
flowers to the foot of the stage.

Don't Forget to Breathe

Believe me—
It's going to be okay.

He's not going to stay
And he may not come back
But it has nothing to do
With anything that you lack.
He's just an ass
And some things don't last,
So just let him leave
But please...

Don't forget to
Breathe.

He may not care
That you've always
Been there
Helping him through.
He sees only the things
You're unable to do.
So,
Don't let his blindness for life
Stifle you.
Open that door
—Not for him,
But for you
And please...

Don't forget to
Breathe.

He wants you
To plead for him
Down on your knees

—But don't give it to him.

He wants you
To cry and ask
Why baby why?

—But don't give in to him.

He will still say
   Bye-bye
And leave you
Alone,
Hoping you're
Pining for him by the phone—

Writing sad poetry,
Singing sad songs
About how much you hurt
About how much you grieve
About how,
Since he's broken your heart,
You can't breathe

—But don't do it for him.

Don't stand in his way—
Help the fool pack!
Remember *HIS* faults
And how much *HE* lacks.
It's the end of an act,
Not the end of your show.

Let him go!
        But please,

Don't let him leave
Without first letting him
See you...

            ...BREATHE!

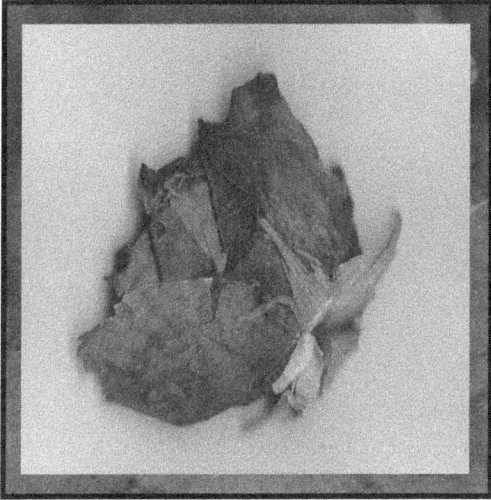

ABOUT THE AUTHOR

Cedric L. Jones writes poetry, drama, and the occasional comedy sketch. He is the author of three books of poetry: *I Wear the Colour Green, We Whisper and Other Poems*, and *Today, I Found This Rose*. He was named the 2000 Emerald Theatre Best Play Award recipient, as well as a finalist for the Manhattan Theatre Source 12th Annual EstroGenius Festival. His short plays *Verses* and *Trouble in Paradise* were performed in Manhattan as part of the 10th Annual Midtown International Play Festival under the collected title *Bible Stories*. In addition to writing, he enjoys acting and performing as the vocalist with the jazz trio *Mister Diva & The Gents*.

ABOUT THESPIS

Legend has it that the poet Thespis was the first person to step away from the Greek Chorus and to assume a dramatic character. In the role of Dionysus, God of wine and theater, he became the first actor, or *thespian*.

ALSO BY CEDRIC L. JONES

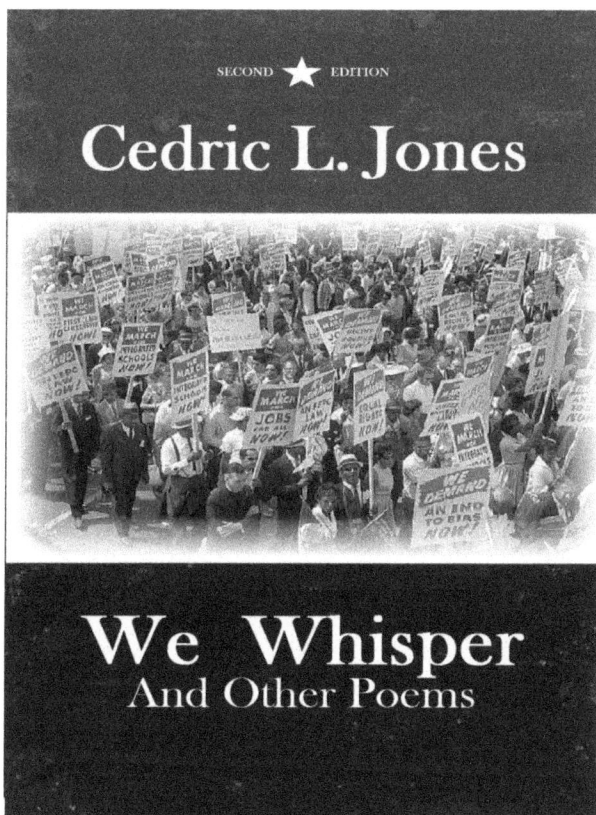

We Whisper
And Other Poems